OSTRACIZED

Abuse on our family trees

Juss Shy Ofproof

Dedication

To all of the survivors, who have shown the courage, strength, and endurance, to speak up on behalf of the "voiceless," I applaud you for giving voice and action to many forms of abuse. Now we must advocate for legislation and punishment for the perpetrator(s) that is commensurate to a survivor's sentence—life.

So, you ostracize me?

Because I tell you what I see

I've seen things with my own eyes

People will say, don't believe her

She is always telling lies

Let us just ignore her

And look the other way

No matter what she continues to say

We will reject her love and her presence each day

Pretend there is no truth

Because there is no proof

Let's pretend that she is lying and blind

It's just her words against mine

No one will believe her over me

Just deny it, you will see

Let's carry on being fancy and free

People say, don't believe your ears nor eyes

If you do, you will be ostracized

Say she didn't see, what she said she saw

Doing what I did—was it breaking the law?

Who is to say-- What I did may not have been
morally right?

If I admit the truth, it will only cause a fight

I will continue to spread my love, affection, and
charm

But admitting the truth, my reputation will be
harmed

Who cares anyway, it was only a touch

What I did--it wasn't all that much

I will stick to my initial lies

It will never show in my eyes

I'll pretend that it wasn't me

But you will be ostracized

Just you wait and see

It's your word against mine

I will pretend as if everything is fine

"Whatever" says the violator— "You will see

They will call you a liar; and they will believe me

So, what if I was on top of you - You didn't mind

We were just playing, it wasn't a crime

If I rubbed your chest, breast, or thighs,

I know you enjoyed it

I could tell by your eyes

If I was wrong, you should have said stop

I was on the bottom and you were on top

No matter what you think or what you're going to say

I'll just say, we were wrestling and in the middle of play."

Generation after generation, this appears to be okay

For some crazy reason, it just seems to be that way

I used to be asked, what was wrong and what has happened to me

But then people would wave me off, and say, you were only 3

Just forget about it; it's all in the past

How long does the memory, hurt, and pain last?

Where do you feel safe when it's a stranger, family member, or a friend?

Who says, 'you better not tell' at the very end

No one will ever believe me because I have no proof

My violator will just say, "You're not telling the truth."

Walking home, feeling violated and sad

My loved ones are acting like I did something bad

They asked questions like, "Did you wear that outfit or go over there?

You just got that dress, and now it has a tear."

The mangled dress and my appearance were their only care

Then I was told, "Why don't you fix your hair?"

OSTRACIZED

"Go get a needle and thread," my mom said,

"I should knock you upside your head

This wouldn't have happened had you listened to me

You have been lying and crying ever since you were three.

You accused the neighbor of kissing you on the lips

Why would he kiss a little girl that wasn't even 6?

Go to bed and get out of my face

While I sew your ripped panty lace

You make me sick; you are always running your mouth

Get your stuff together so we can get ready to go down South."

More fright begins to set in as I think about this trip

How do I avoid the awaiting monster's vicious grip?

As we reached the southern town, and the adults were about to leave

The perpetrator took my little arms out of my shirt sleeve

Rubbing my stomach and my tiny chest

Even when I have no breast

What do I do? No one will ever hear me yell

Dear GOD in heaven, who do I tell?

OSTRACIZED

If I tell, I will be called a liar, a whore, and a slut

Now at age 7, he's rubbing my little butt

How was I to know that was an orgasm

I couldn't identify that visceral spasm

Where do I go in order to feel safe--

on vacation, to the neighbors, or some other place?

Time continues to be filled with violation and abuse

I say **GOD**, Oh **GOD**, what's the use?

One day, I had a stalker, who declared he would
never do me wrong or harm

Now how do I explain this 6-inch gash on my arm?

"Keep your mouth shut" he said, "telling your
stories and lies

You think your family loves you?

You will be ostracized

They will no longer want you around"

As I was violently thrown to the ground

Scared to death, and seeing the shiny gun,

The perpetrator said, "Let's have some fun."

Fright was an understatement; I could hardly cry

But I promise, I promise, I would not lie

As the gun was placed to my head and this monster
pulled my hair

He said, "hey you stupid bitch, who do you think
will really care?"

I just thought, who's going to help me?

As I felt such despair

There will be another beating because he messed up my hair

I used to look forward to the fairytales of all of my "firsts"

But I didn't realize my firsts would be my worst

How special is it to lose your virginity on a dining room floor?

The only thing the perpetrator said, "I'll be back for more."

Where will my life go from here?

My life has entered another level of fear

Impregnated at the young age of 14

I know when I tell the family; they will rage and scream

It had to have been that mini-dress

Or was it "my little hot ass" which caused this mess

Placing the leaf of shame on the family tree

Being that I was being called, a "fast ass," ever since I was three

The silence becomes deafening as I was ostracized

As the many paths of abuse seemed to multiply

There will be no special first kiss, first dance, or first date

Because in words of my loved ones, my "fast ass" couldn't wait

As if the unprovoked Russian roulette game wasn't enough

Now, here comes the other stuff

The gun play, the beating with people's fists and belts

My "special firsts" are filled with emotional scars and physical welts

It wasn't the perpetrator's fault, he just took my
first kiss

So, what, if I was just three or four

I shouldn't have gone on his porch or to the candy
store

It wasn't the perpetrator's fault

who fondled me or rubbed my little chest

Maybe, it was the color of my favorite dress

It wasn't the perpetrator's fault, who gave me my
first orgasm at 7

or the loss of my virginity though I was just over 11

Where do I go--which way do I turn?

How do I suppose to learn?

It wasn't the perpetrator's fault who put the gun to
my head

had to be those shorts and jacket, all tight and red

It wasn't the perpetrator's fault, who impregnated
me as I was a 14-year-old kid

People blamed me—it had to be the things that I did

Oh Lord, you said, I can have faith in you

But what in the world am I supposed to do?

I'm causing trouble and they say I'm full of lies

One by one, I have become more and more
ostracized

"You will never be anything," my abuser(s) often
said

Now, it's like a ticker tape inside my head

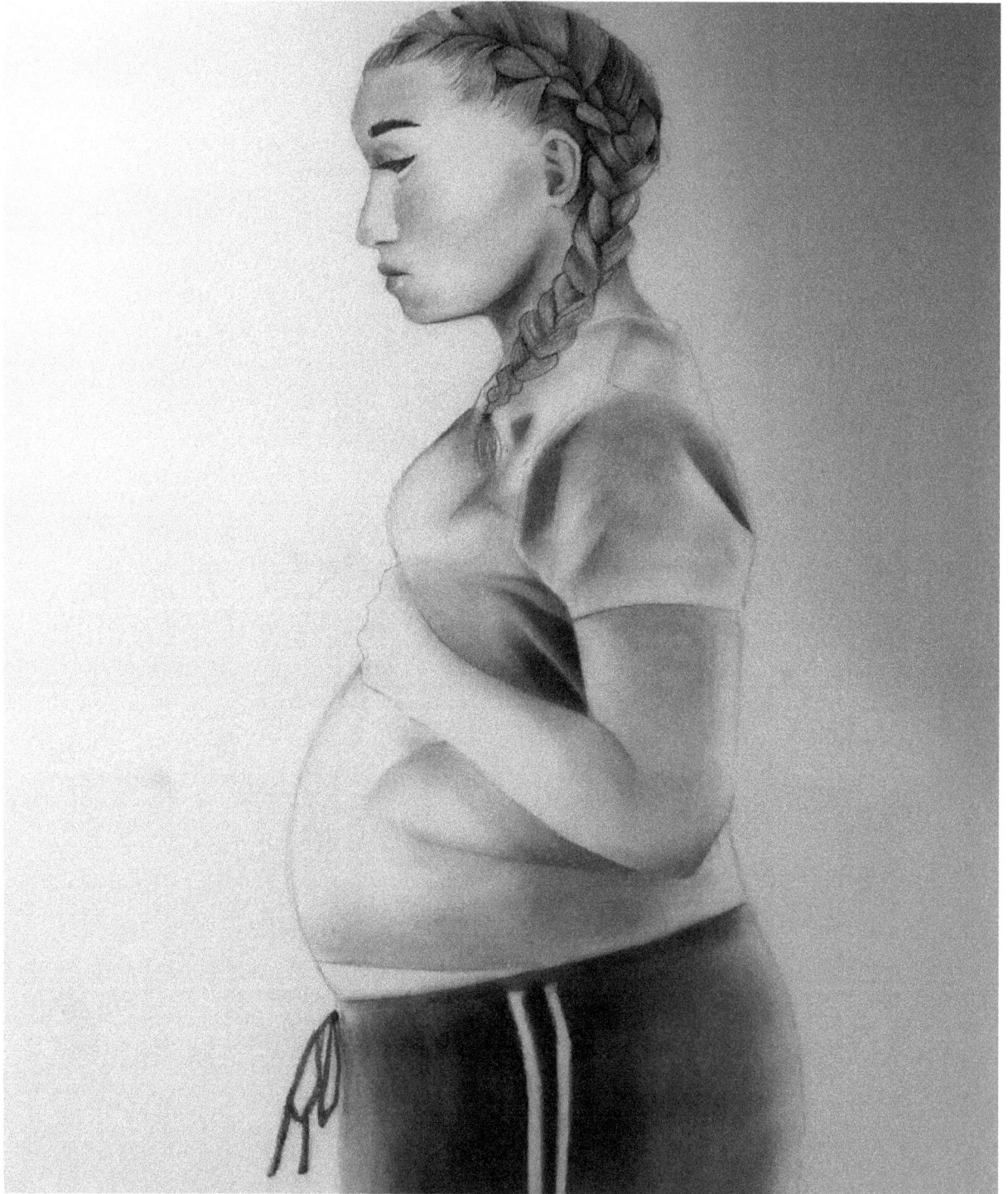

OSTRACIZED

God, you told me to please have faith, and I would be okay

You said that I would be able to help others, who were treated in the same way

I guess all of the abuse gave me purpose in life

causing many bad dreams and decades of strife

I refuse to let these experiences define and defeat me

I know what I know, and I know what I see

I will not let these stains define who I am

Or blame every person or every man

My inner strength, my spiritual belief,

have given me a level of unexplainable relief

Does the abuser continue to abuse?

My thoughts as I ponder and muse

Please GOD--can you give me an answer-- what is this?

Why do people batter one another with weapons and their fists?

I don't have the answer, it is such a mystery to me

But it isn't only on my family's tree

It's all around us but we just turn our heads

Domestic violence and abuse have left many stains and many dead

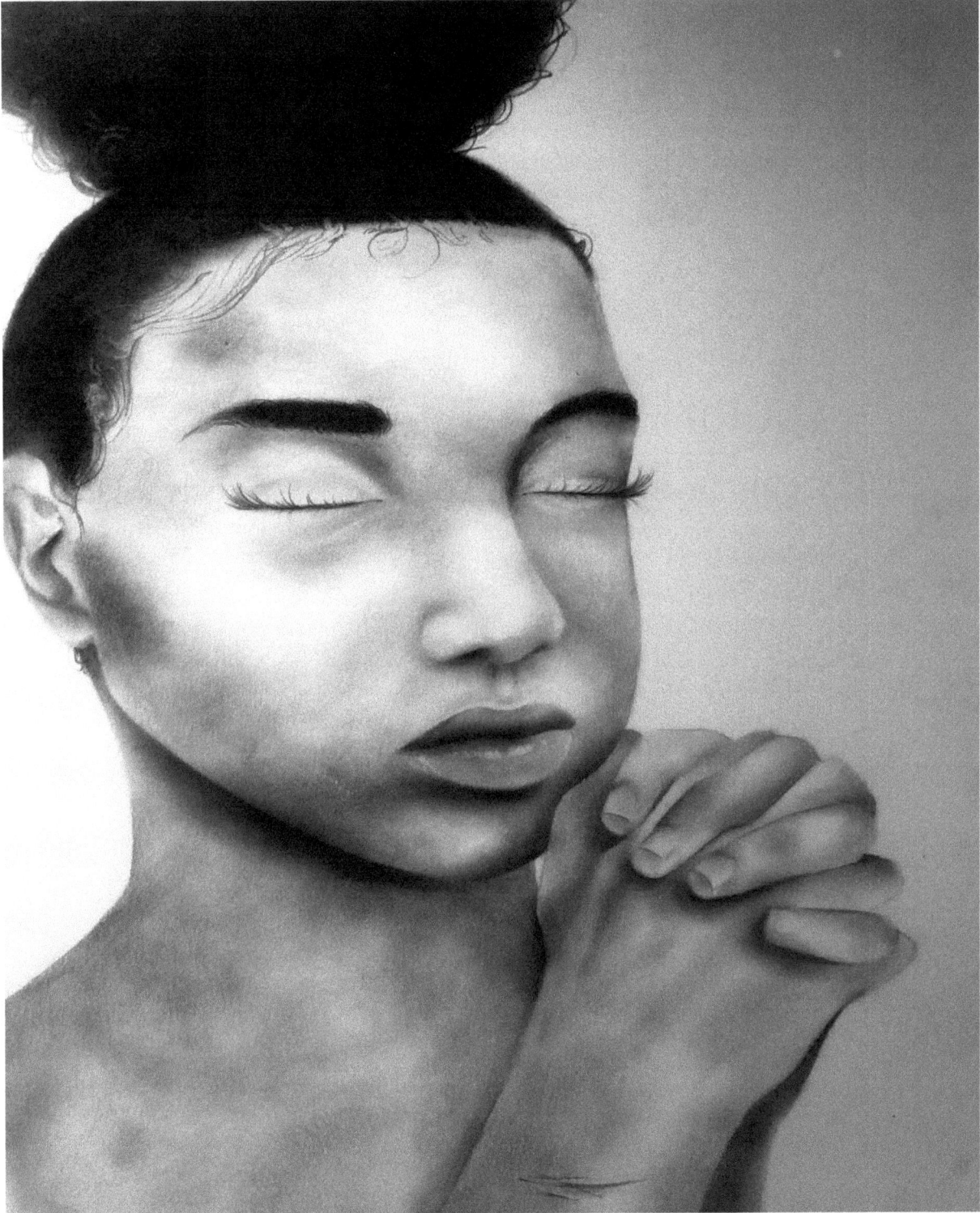

OSTRACIZED

Are there answers that I can find?

Why can't we make an effort to be more kind?

I refuse to stop talking about the things that we all
see

Even if it means they will ostracize me

But I say GOD, you told me that I'd be okay

Please help me and others not be treated in this way

Let me know that you are here with us

Your grace and mercy are definitely a plus

You told me that you are giving me this hour

In order to share my experiences and help to empower

I believe what you told me a long time ago

I know how it feels, and I know what I know

I recall the rumors started a long time ago

It started with people I didn't even know

One was a woman whose name was Ida Mae

family and friends would repeatedly say

She was thrown from a place that was really high

Out of her apartment window as if she could fly

I never met her but I felt that her spirit lived on

Hearing her life story began to make me strong

It didn't stop there; I had a cousin, too

whose mate locked her in a closet beaten black and blue

She had a bloody face and bloody eyes

He called her names, and said, she was unloved and despised

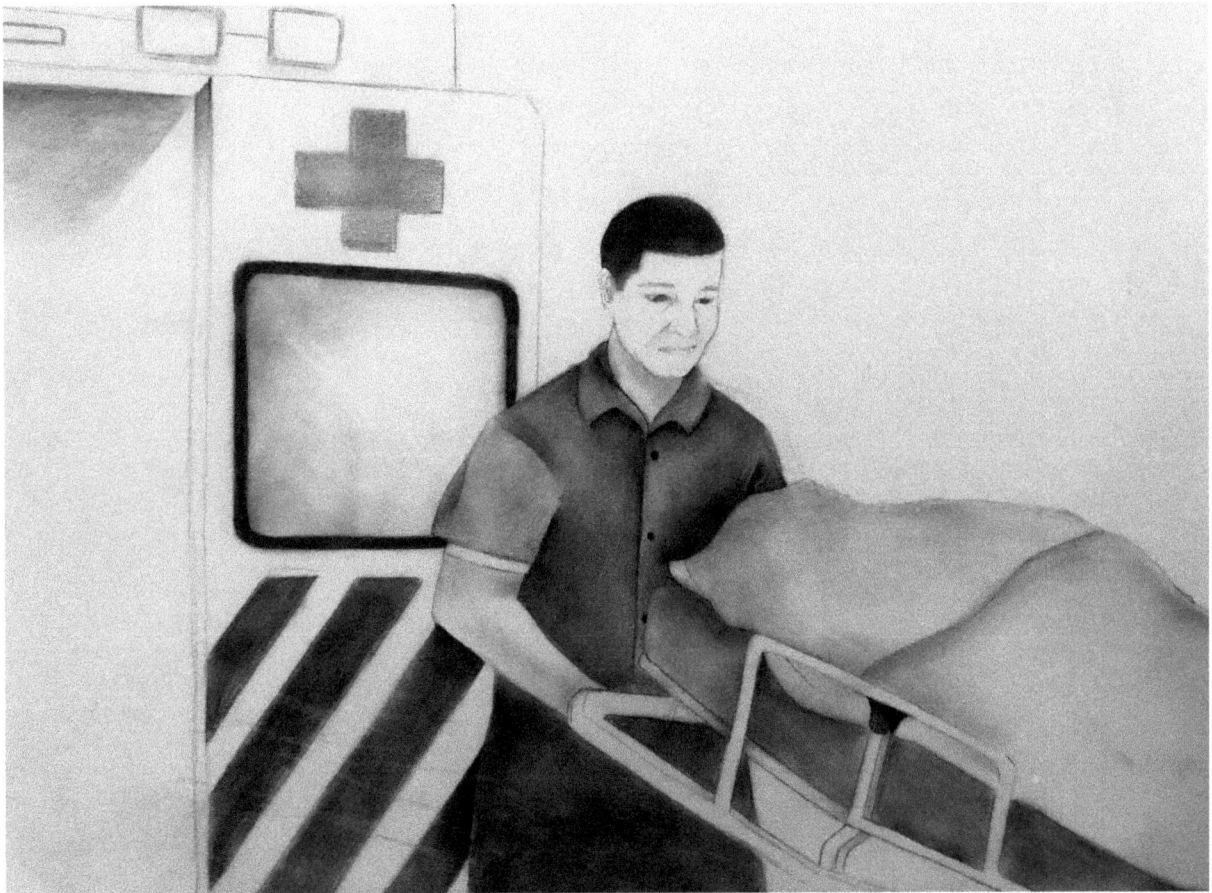

OSTRACIZED

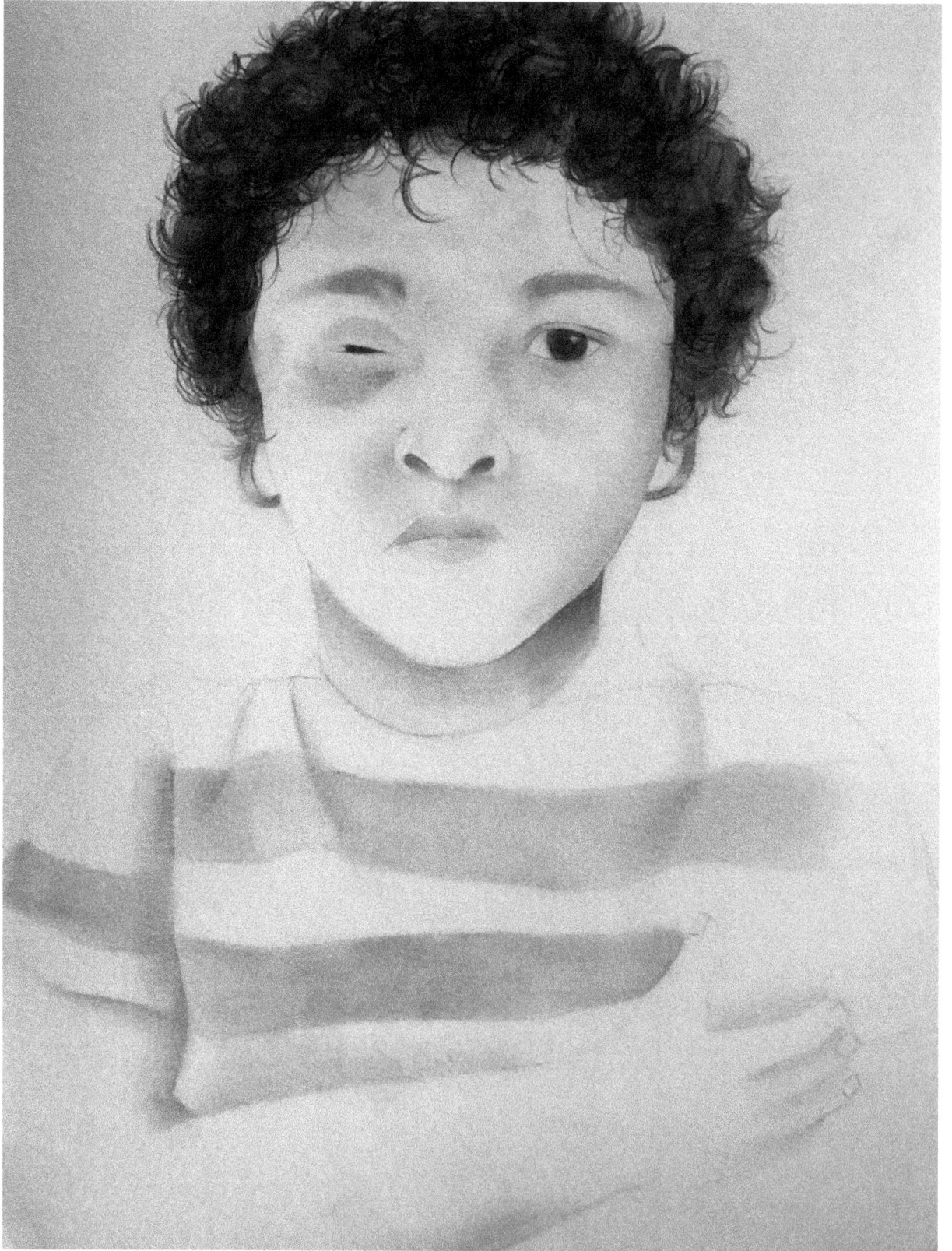

Juss Shy Ofproof

OSTRACIZED

I always heard that my grandmother's leg was broken by a man

Most days I saw her, she could barely stand

She persevered and never complained--not one day

Please don't come back--is what I used pray

It continues on all of our families' trees

My granny, my auntie, my cousin, and me

What would be on the leaves of your family's tree?

Some of us pick the same kind of mate

Saying, "I'm in love," as the mate exhibits violence and hate

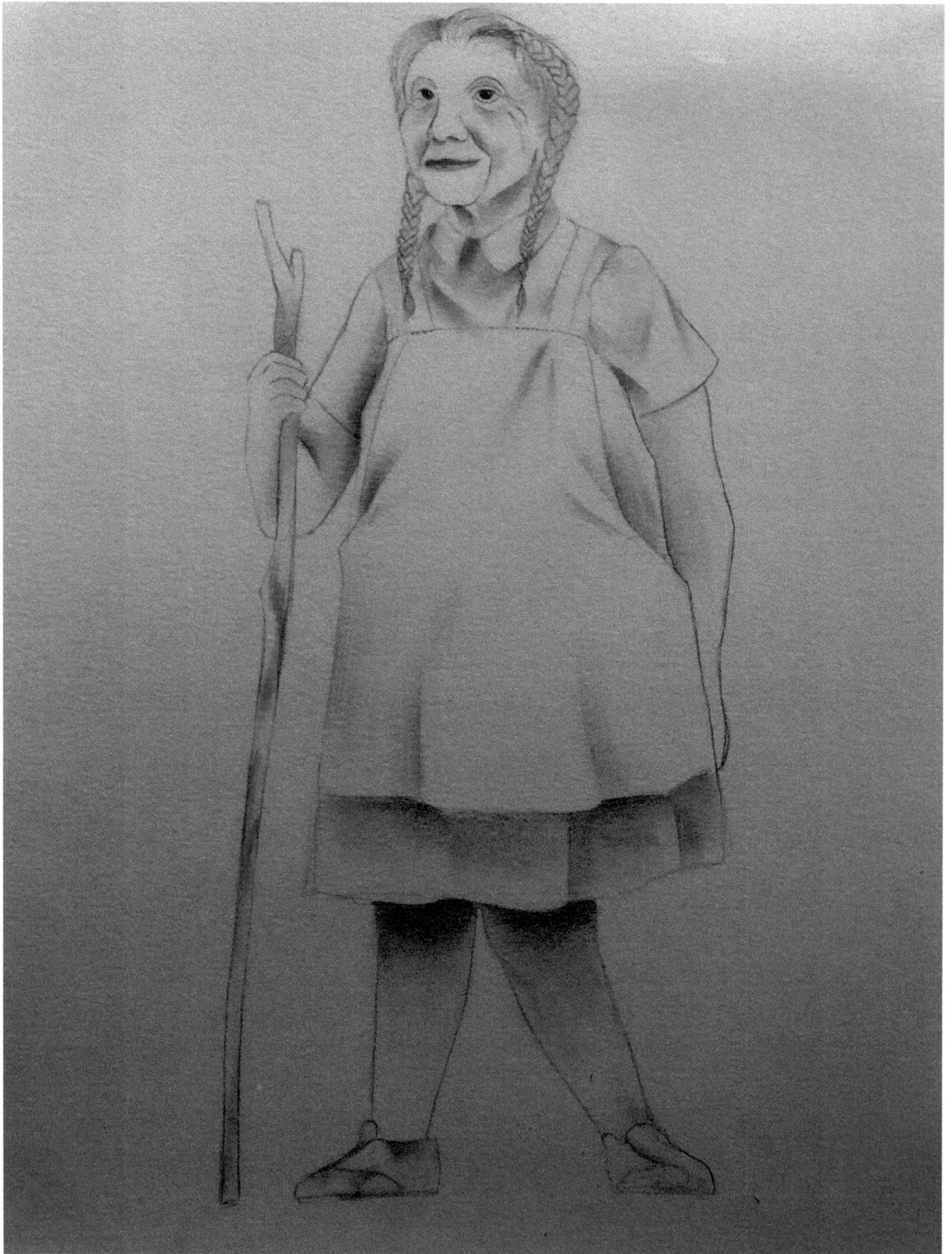

Juss Shy Ofproof

OSTRACIZED

If we are truthful about our family trees, imagine all
the damaged roots, branches, and leaves

Stopping the violence is surely a must

Violence serves no purpose as it's inflicted upon us

So much of our society sees the signs

Yet we turn our heads and pretend to be blind

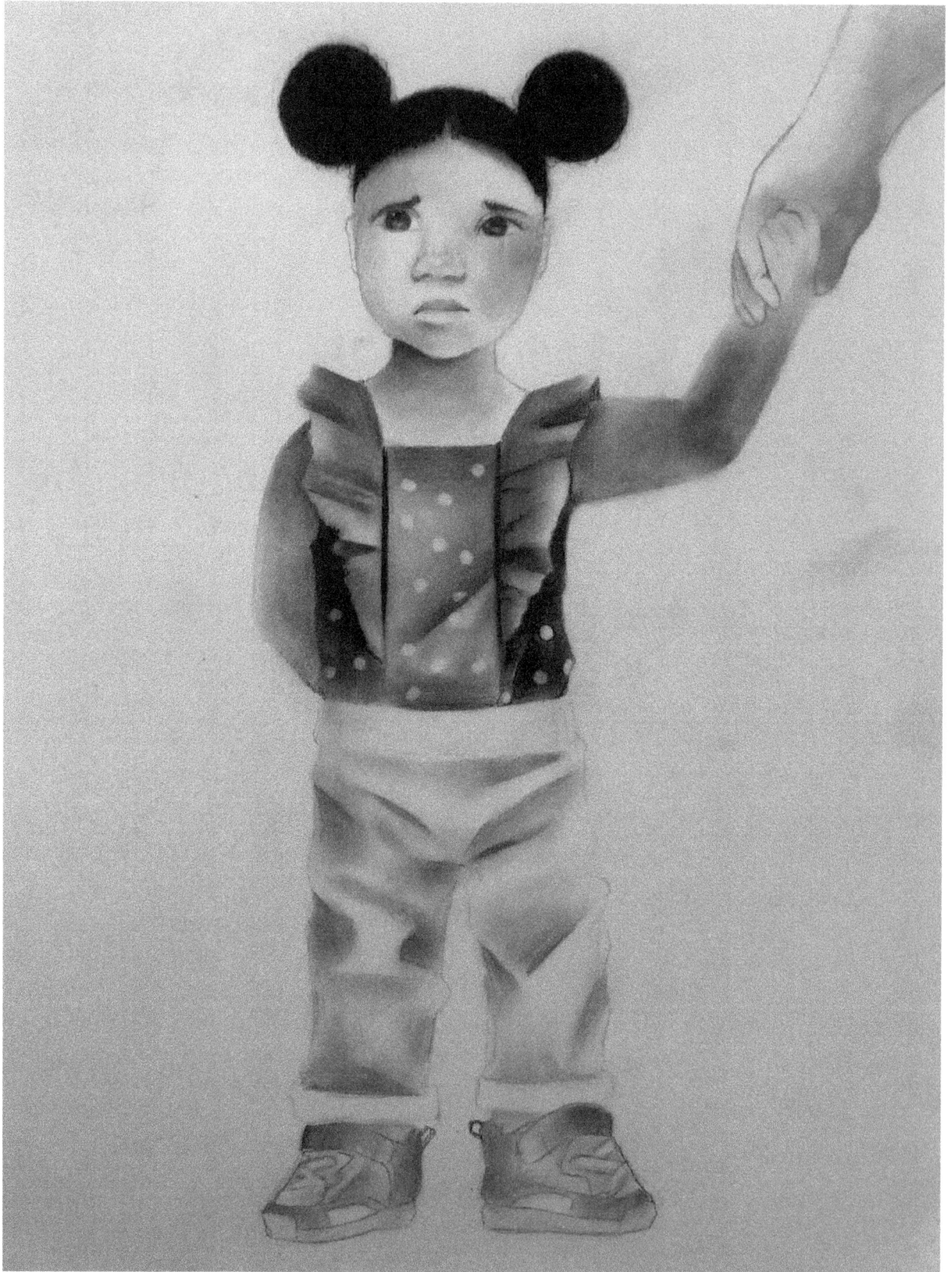

OSTRACIZED

Our teachers, our police, and our clergy, too

They don't want to witness the evident abuse

I can only think about what has happened to me

Sometimes I wonder if it is like having PTSD

A person, a place, or a thing can really trigger me

Juss Shy Ofproof

OSTRACIZED

GOD, my comfort comes in faith

That my life experiences will not be a waste

Though, I may not have obvious, physical proof

Those who choose not to believe me will never quash
my truth

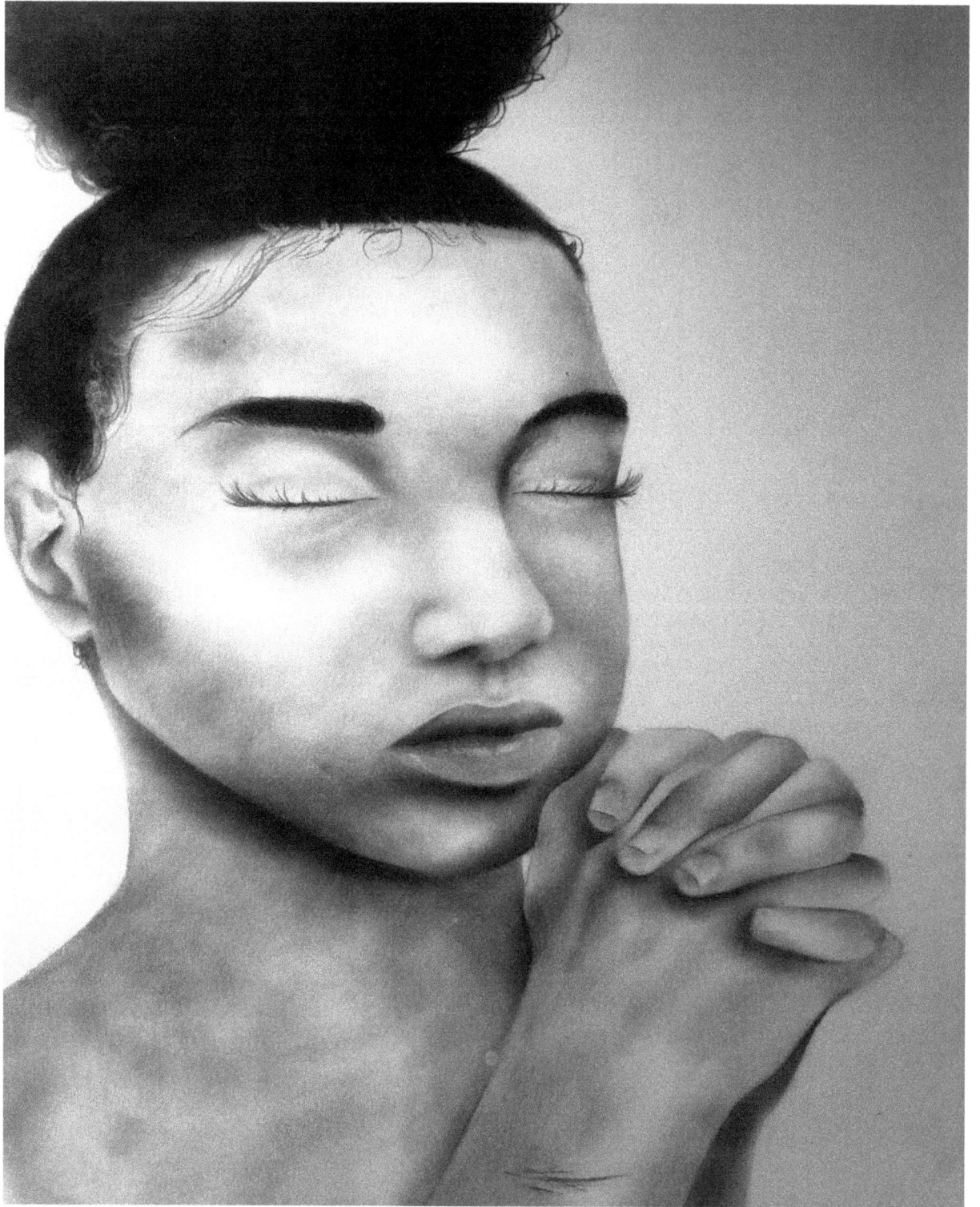

Juss Shy Ofproof

OSTRACIZED

Although I can only try to open other people's eyes

Hopefully, my story will make others wise

I will speak on behalf of the "voiceless" and others
who have died

Even if it means, I will be shunned or ostracized,
ostracized, ostracized.

National Domestic Violence Hotline

- **1-800-799-7233 (SAFE)**

- **1-800-787-3244 (TTY)**

- **THE NATIONAL COALITION AGAINST DOMESTIC VIOLENCE (NCADV)**

NCADV's 20th National Conference on Domestic Violence

September 19th-21st, 2021

Capitol Hill Day is September 22nd, 2021

April Is National Child Abuse Prevention Month

https://nationalchildabusecoalition.org

National Child Abuse Coalition Members

If you know someone who is in trouble or needs assistance, call the Child Help National Child Abuse Hotline at 1-800-4-A-Child (1-800-422-4453)

A special thank you to **Daesha Y.** and **Sandra G.** for your creative spirits. Thank you for helping me to convey my message via your beautiful artistry.

Author's Bio

Raised in the south and a graduate of a prestigious HBCU, Juss Shy Ofproof, has worked in the legal and rehabilitative fields. She has been an advocate for women, children, and the "voiceless."

She has taken on a crusade to bring awareness of issues that continue to plague our society such as bullying and abuse.

Her books and game apps, Bella and Team Tutu, What's Wrong With Wallee and Wheezee?, Space Searches for Grandma-ma's Smile, and her future works will address issues that positively and negatively affect our children, our youth, and our society.

Visit https://11stainedtutus.net or e-mail me at jussshyofproof2020@gmail.com

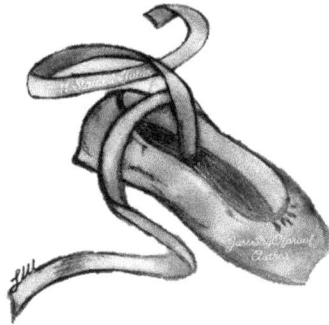

OSTRACIZED

www.ingramcontent.com/pod-product-compliance
Lightning Source LLC
Chambersburg PA
CBHW040302100426
42811CB00011B/1340